Publish on Demand, Inc.
© Fylatos Publishing,
Thessaloniki & Delaware 2019
Author: Rania Angelakoudi
Editor: Konstantinos Fylatos

Republication of parts of this work is permitted for comment or criticism. Republication of a limited part of this work is permitted for scientific purposes. Reference to the title of the work, the name of the author, publisher, number of the page republished and date of publication is mandatory. Any revision, translation or utilisation is prohibited without reference to the book's contributors and written permission from the publisher according to the law.

© Fylatos Publishing
e-mail: contact@fylatos.com
web: www.fylatos.com

Pagination-Design: © Fylatos Publishing
ISBN: 978-618-5318-66-6

Rania Angelakoudi

On Pomegranate Lanes

Fylatos Publishing
Thessaloniki & Delaware
2019

Contents

A FEW WORDS ABOUT THE AUTHOR…	6
STENTORIAN RADIANCE	11
TEMPEST	12
THE ADVENT OF YOUR BLOSSOM	13
THE COLORS OF YOUR LAKE	14
WHEN I SPEAK OF YOU	15
A NIGHT IN PRAYER	16
A PLEDGE	17
A SENSE OF WAITING	18
A WORLD OF YOU	19
CERTAIN SUNDAYS	20
BEYOND BORDERS	22
CITY LIGHTS	23
DREAM MAIDEN	24
EUTOPIA	25
I WANT YOU TO KNOW	26
IMPRINT	27
IN YOUR DEEP BLUE WATERS	28
INDELIBLE SUMMERS	29
INVIGORATING NEED	30
LOVE EFFERVESCENT	31
LOVE'S GAZE	32
MAKE HASTE!	33
MERCILESS	34
OBLITERATING TIME	35
ON POMEGRANATE LANES	36
PRIESTESS	37
QUEST	38
RESOLUTION	39
RUGGED ROAD	40
SHELTERING SKY	41

A few words about the Author...

Rania Angelakoudi was born in Kronanberg, Sweden a city she still visits and has close ties with. She's been a citizen of the world from an early age, travelling and meeting people, sharing ideas and experiences with other artists about life, human affairs and Mother Nature, a subject close to her heart.

Her English Language studies have allowed her to study, explore and inspired by the international literary scene.

She currently works as an English Language teacher, dividing her time between her students and her two favourite pastimes, painting and primarily poetry.

She has published poems in Greek and International Literary Journals receiving positive comments. This encouraged her to participate in various literary competitions where a number of her poems have received praise and awards.

In 2013 her poem "Orfic rite" came third among hundreds of participating poems from Greece and Cyprus in a competition organized by the Municipality of Evosmos, Thessaloniki under the auspices of the Greek Ministry of Culture.

In 2014 her poem "Pomegranate Tree Lane" won the bronze metal in a European Literary Competition organized by the Municipality of Kessaria Kozani and the Vafopoulio Cultural Centre of Thessaloniki.

In 2015 her poem "Of Human Affairs" translated in the Italian Language with the title 'Rapporti Umani'came third in an international competition making Rania the first Greek poet to be awarded a distinction by the PiGrecoZen corporation under the auspices of the Italian Ministry of culture and the Municipality of Ankona. The special ceremony took part at Museo della citta.

In 2016 her poem "In Shallow waters" came fifth among a number of entries from London, Germany, Greek, and Cyprus during the 9th meeting of Contemporary Artists held by the Literary Journal "Pnoes Logou". She has also contributed work to the collection of poems "In the city of ideas" along with other distinguished poets and in the anthology "A Poets Fest" published by Orion Publications. Her poems can also be found in the anthology "Oh Love" by Bergina Publications and the Literary Journal "Keleno". The international magazine "Our Poetry Archive" announced her among the 10 top Poets in Europe publishing her poems in September's 2016 issue and among the 30 top Poets in the world.The Literary Journal «Atunis» based on Brussels has also present her as a distinguished Poetess. A number of her poems can be found in Setu magazine based on Pittsburgh USA as well.

The humanitarian organization World Institute for Peace nominated her to receive the prestigious award the "Icon For World Peace" in November 2016 for the active participation and popularity of her poetical work for Peace in the world. The same organization honourably announced her Ambassador of W.I.P for Greek and Swedish branches.

In January 2017 the Association of Journalists for Tourism EDSTE announced her to become a member in honour to her International success.

In August 2017 she was honorably invited to international poetry festival to represent her both countries Greece and Sweden in Hyderabat India and in April the same year in Singapore.

Her books are found in the central libraries in Stockholm at Stadsbiblioteket and Kulturhuset bibliotek. In December 2017 another important nomination announced her with the title "Pride of the Globe"-2017, WNWU for her devotion to literature for a better picture of the world.

In February 2018 the council of World Institute for Peace decided to reannounced her the title of Ambassador for Greece and Swedish brances as a permanent representative.

In November 2018 the historical union Verbumlandi Art based in Italy awarded her for her poem 'Oblitarating Time' among a number of international entries.

*I expect this collection to be
the headrest to touch the fragile hearts.
I hope to be the lighthouse
of warmth during the flert with love.
A gulp of hope that escaped from the desert.
A lightning of your soul's rise.
For me is an ode to love and life.*

Stentorian Radiance

Be still! Await a while my steps to heed,
the ones that lead to you!
Hold still! My heavy breath no longer stands
to trail behind your thoughts
to overtake wild throbs!
Throbs of yearning... yearning to conjoin
To swirl and spin....to twirl and blend...
Like raindrops merging with the river flow.
Hold still! That I may embrace you
while your life-giving gaze leads me
to happiness unbound...to happiness untamed!
Hold still! My steps thither I have traced...
To the stentorian radiance of your existence
To the stentorian might of your love!

Tempest

Insufferable the city seemed
shrouded in its gray beauty,
smog from the buses
and shouts from the marches.
A space closed off like a bubble
we are like animals in a jungle
bitter voices...empty promises...
a rampant rabble!
Then you like a tempest came
sweeping everything in your stride,
and the jungle became a meadow
the rabble a caress
the gray became a mirror
the city changed its dress
life its sail sets!

The advent of your blossom

Once you came, my bruises into blossoms turned!
You came...And the rusty beatings of my heart
to sound like melodies began!
Yes, you came!
And I navigate my life through the sea routes of your eyes...
In your crystal blue embrace,
The troubled world I dream over
You came!... On my dreams tenderly you tread,
with your love you obliterate my life mistakes.
I am alive!...when you hold your hand in mine.
I feel alive when your velvet lips touch mine!
I clearly see... how it all begins anew,
To broken words you give shape
Yes!...the time for love to thrive came!

The colors of your lake

I fell in love with the colors of your lake,
water lilies dancing in the wave...
My hands into your waters longingly I dipped
some droplets onto my dry scorched lips to bring!
Your Doric form reflected
into my cupped hands
Smiling like Narcissus
as it stands!
Playing tricks with the water
as it blends!

And then, one with the drops
I become!
A water lily swinging
in the wave!
A color from the much
beloved lake!
A fairy in the sky
flying away!

When I speak of you

I speak of you as of a silver shower
while I, a garden parched,
await for your downpour with hands outstretched.
I dream of fragrant shrubberies
of lilies rare...
The ones your rain envelops
As they spread out and loom large!

I speak of you as of a sweet sensation
that spreads with eventide
in the luminous trails of Zephyrus.
Our caress blazes trough the night.
I speak of you and I cry out
for your love!
Rumble and thunder
pierce the air with your name
This name,
This downpour,
This eventide,
The caress my life
embroidered on my skin...
thus I became your garden
my precious rain!

A night in prayer

Spend the night in prayer
until the day breaks
the gift of dawn awaits!
Wear it like a robe
so that you stand out
in ancient markets as you roam!
Red lips warm kiss
a glass of sweet wine
your scarf waving
in the rainy breeze
but you won't leave!
The north wind I bribed
in safe ports to keep you stranded!
Oblation solemn did I make
the scent of incense in your wake,
in every step you take....wherever you may be...
But you won't leave!

A Pledge

My arms with flowers
shall I fill
And the gods of dreams shall I beseech
once you sleep to clear the sky
so your dreams may fill with light;
a thousand moons to shine bright
your steps that I may follow through the night
and the wind to stay still
your breasts that I may hear heave.
And when my gaze
your own meets
the war of the elements will cease.
For your golden hair shall I weave
a garland of lilies white
your soul to fill with notes and scents
your life forever to delight.
And if ever sorrow knocks on your door
your hand in mine
shall I firmly hold.

A sense of waiting

The northern lights shall I wait
the sky to illuminate...
And the birds to be guide
as I try you to find...
Till the morrow shall I hold
your scent in my embrace
while at night your body's throbs
in my mind I encase!
And, so my love, the night wears on
and a new dream with you
begins at dawn!
How beautiful the day breaks
when I have you in my embrace!

A World of You

I meant to pick roses for you,
But you surpassed their beauty!
I set my sights on wildflowers instead
but their hues faded in your presence!
I meant a few words to write...
But they fell short of describing you.
I meant colors to blend but you outshone them all!
I meant to offer you the world,
but I realized that the whole wide world is you....
And so I found myself embracing the world!

Certain Sundays

On certain Sundays
the birds on the street
our joy welcomed...
It was spring then!
I shall never forget the musings
with the lapping shore
the song that together we heard...
But it was spring then!
The wildflowers spraying
their fragrance everywhere and the grass
spreading its arms
to you and me...
It was spring full blown!
But winter too was spring!
Those winter Sundays
felt like spring
to you and me...
The golden yellow leaves sparkling
sprawled across our paths...
That's where I shall go to sprinkle them
with the dew from my eyes...
For thus shall I hold on to
the winters and spring alike.
For I can let my tears
flow...
I am not afraid...
Yes! I shall never forget the winter Sundays
that felt like spring
to you and me...
When birds would sing
through nights everlasting
when the Skies would wear their best

to welcome us...
The logs on the fire struggling
our gazes to keep warm
and all of nature swathed in light...
For you and me.
Once it was spring
with you and me!

Beyond borders

Life knows no borders...
Barbed wires hurt me
Because I was born Free!
My life...resembles the sea,
And like a sea it stretches
Enveloping my mother
The Earth!...and my Brothers!
Who live scattered under the sun.

Life knows no borders....
Because I was born to live
Free!
To love!
To breath!
To create!
To conquer!
To share!
To dream!
To carry on!
And dance the dance of peace.

Because life knows no borders....
Because barbed wires hurt me!
Because my brothers
live scattered far and wide,
because I was born Free
and Free I shall remain!
Dancing the dance of peace
alongside my brothers
who live scattered near and far....
Because we are Free!

City lights

The city lights shine bright
like colorful candles
as the rain begins to fall
I'm all alone
through the echoes
of the route announced
forever on hold!

An excerpt by Marquez
a nuanced text,
from an old newspaper
turned on the last page
a yellowish haze!
A blurry landscape in the mist
and you, a form of silent appeal,
an unrelenting need,
an unknown route about to begin.
Endless kilometers
along the road's barometers!

Dream maiden

Dream maiden, goddess beloved
your throne I set deep in my soul
the world comes alive by the light of your eyes
Nature blossoms and dances.
I bathe in the torrent of your hair
and my soul into your arms spreads,
a threshold to a soaring of emotions,
a threshold to a world of dreams
graced by the songs of muses,
melodies from harps and Pan's flute as
accompaniment.
Like a siren you enchanted me
and held me close to you, my fair city
to live in a world of reverie
and to forego my Ulyssean adventures
in this life and the Clashing Rocks
that stand in my way...
And like a dove you lead me onwards ...
Away from the rocks and like a star
you shine the way until I come
into your arms to lose myself
and so the journey begins anew...
Dream maiden, goddess beloved
City of dreams.

Eutopia

If you love transparent summers
sun-scorched island alleyways
a full moon
in the break of dawn
herbs that intoxicate your senses
and whispers brushing your neck
Then come to me!

If you love swimming
in crystal waters
making your bed
on silver foliage
wrapping yourself
with bird wings
and resting your eyelids
to the lullaby of angels
Then stay with me!

My world is blissful....it awaits you!

I want you to know

Far and wide I travelled
to find you...
This you should know!
Scores of people I met
before you I saw...
I crossed oceans
I carved roads on clouds...
In thunder and storm
your form became my shield!
You ought to know!
Hostile lands I made my home
I drank water from the seas
my thirst to quench...
This you should know!
Hope wrapped up my body
keeping it warm at night...
The stars were my guide...
but their light flickered!
A handful of joy
dispersed in the air...
A tear hung around my neck
A smile buried in sweltering heat
I want you to know!
I caught a glimpse of your radiance through the haze
and, with bated breath,
I met your limpid gaze
and into your waters I rushed to plunge
of my ceaseless wanderings
to wash off the mud.
This, you should know!
I want you to know!

Imprint

The world I traveled far and wide
your traces I could not find.
Over the lakes where you tread
the lakes where you stargaze,
a flock of herons shall I send
their broad winds wide to spread
a dome to form
so you may stand
under its shade
the sky...the colors
and the world to contemplate,
a sprite eternal on a throne
the world to ordain!
Thereabouts shall I roam
near your imprint ...
Near the lakes where you tread
the lakes where you stargaze
a sprite eternal on a throne
the world ordains!

In Your Deep Blue Waters

In your deep blue waters my dreams
I baptized!
Land of oracles and philosophers,
land of light...mother of intellect
in your deep blue waters Gods were born.
In your bosom they were nurtured
and grew fierce.

And the mortals they infused with knowledge,
high and low.
And under their watchful eye
justice was safeguarded.

In your deep blue waters
young lads shed their blood.
They wrapped their bodies with the robe of death!
Love dived in your deep blue waters
and life emerged as the daughter of beauty!
To bask in your sun,
to study and ordain human endeavor.
From your deep blue waters
dream on earth sprang and knowledge
became the Wealth of the world
and a torch burning
to the end of time
Far and wide.
In your deep blue waters every morning
the sun is reflected and I...
and I...gaze at your blue
and carry on...and carry on....

Indelible summers

All the memories of summers past
in stone shall I carve
indelible to keep.
Not a beat from the waves
lapping on the shore
to be forgot...
All the memories of the summer new
alive with my pen
shall I keep,
the book of life with blue
I aim to fill
so the sea will always carry me
to your shores
in breezy summers!

Invigorating need

My heart stands still
in your presence!
Reverent are the hours that virtues become
and set sail on the vessel of my love.
The sky remolds the world for you,
injecting hues in colorless things
reshaping the clouds
to form a rainbow smile...
My love invigorating
will enfold you...
It will blossom for you!
Open wide the blinds of your soul
remove your bolts
the torrent of my passion
all around you
will be raging.

Love Effervescent

I hum a tune, that's what I do!
Coarse words, I have erased
Words that had become blades.
The scars from my burning tears healed!
My bosom swelled with rupture...
You bestow on me the blossoms of your bliss!
The naked line of painful memories has been
immortalized ...
Now, life bears the hue of flames,
Passion carries the blaze of light...
My soul finally has a voice because your breath
exudes love effervescent!
Now the wind has carved your name on my chest...
Now time is set to everlasting Dawn...
Where together our gazes will roam!

Love's gaze

How can I but gaze on you
when life 's reflected in the sparkle of your eyes?
How can I but long for night to come by my side
bearing your form?
You embrace me like a starry night!
An orchard of love and a forest of affection
I shall have ready for you by daylight.
It may have taken long for our dreams to meet,
but the cloud of bitterness disperses
in the light of our boundless sunrises.
A picture drawn by angels
A song by sirens sung!
Thus shall I gaze on you!

Make haste!

I was picking up scattered words
trying to give them shape...
They escaped....restless as they were...
So, I picked up my gasps for air
my trembling feet
the soaring flames of my soul
and in the two loving hands I dreamed
of willowy fingers entwined with mine
I let my body dissolve
submerged in an ocean of desire
and seeking.
The fragrance of your body pleasure brings
Let us dance to love's melodious tempo
Birds will be chirping at our ball...
Make haste!
Like a blazing sphere you should appear...
Make haste!
Birds will be warbling at our ball!

Merciless

When the song
of your breath stays unheard
night forsakes me.
The hands of the clock stand still
And the tears lash mercilessly
at my cheeks!
Those times when the song
of your breath stays unheard
the dream tears up its pages
and the soul hangs on the heavy chain of its longing
the weight of your absence.
It is unbearable!

Obliterating Time

The earth shall I draw again... and time shall I intoxicate...
Thus shall I obliterate the minutes of your absence
Of sterile seasons, of gloomy days,
Of faceless months!
I shall obliterate the moments when my tears
Swell up!
LIVES without you
Shall I build anew!
Nights devoid of your form
Shall I endure!
Your shadow inescapable in every shade!
Your heart beckoning in every sigh...
Of pleasure!
LIVES devoid of you shall I dream anew
And there I shall reside...
Where your rain falls transparent...
Where your scent from sappy soil ascends!
Where you words sweetly my soul caress!
Where your three-dimensional love unfolds and spreads!
The earth shall I draw again because it is with you alone
I want the recesses of night to roam,
So that you may lead me
To the wide avenues of your kindness
For the LIFE I have devoted to you.

On pomegranate lanes

This is where I shall meet with you, sweet life,
where the spinning-wheel winds its thread
where it weaves its silky tales
where the dewdrops sprinkle your mind
and imagination trails history
across verdant pomegranates lanes!
I shall meet you where Pythia prophesied
And from her oracles you rose
sweet life!
Untamed …Unpredictable!

I shall meet with you there, in the fertile land
of Goddess Demeter,
that we may drink pomegranate juice
and feast on the crops of euphoria!
And we shall taste all the treats
upon earth's bountiful table!
It is there that we shall agree
the cup of peace to fill
our souls to delight
with the essence of fruits
from the fertile blessed land.
That's where I shall get you drunk sweet life!
Untamed!
On verdant pomegranate lanes!

Priestess

A candle I lit in your altar
O Priestess incandescent!
Enveloped as your are in the glow of your goddess
I struggle my eyes to keep open
against the splendor of your light...
It dazzles me!
My respect....
My awe...
My dignity....
And all the riches of my being
I humbly lay at your feet
As you stand tall
Towering...Majestic...Adored
My priestess....Life unpredictable!
My body and soul you have conquered
and all the riches of my being
to you I have bequeathed
and all the riches of my being
to you I shall bequeath
and I shall persevere
and I shall uphold my values
so that with your values they converge
to become ideals
for you and me!
My adored Priestess
Life so beloved and yet so wretched.

Quest

What Icarus gave you his wings
to fly to me?
What Aeolus released the winds
that brought in my arms
you, flower of the Skies,
untouched and untainted?
I swirl around the splendor
of your fragrance.
I thread my way
through the blossomed paths of
your untrodden soul.
In its amorous mazes
I lose myself.
I sway to the vibrations of your heart
in our luminous nights.
When sobs a song become
and tears become music.
To this Icarus shall I yield,
this Aeolus shall I worship.
In your temple a captive shall I remain,
your bonds stoically to endure,
to treasure them
and yearn to live with them.

Resolution

A cup of crystal water
shall I race to bring you
from the springs that together we discovered
where we hid our sighs...
A cup of crystal water
your soul to rejuvenate
the sores from every blaze to heal;
Thither shall I go!
All the colors we saw together
in the break of dawn
as beacons shall I set
our paths to illuminate
until again we meet.
I cannot wait!
Time that ruthlessly
thrashes me to eradicate.
It renders my longing meaningless.
Into the heart of the moon shall I burrow
as night slips into your bed
and daylight will find me softly caressing
your precious dreams
until a silver aura envelops them.
Thither shall I be.

Rugged Road

A long road the fates chose for me
the precious song of love
for you to write...
Each day and night
green leaves to harvest
a hammock to weave for you
your ivory body that you may rest.
This road I shall gladly walk!
If it be rugged
I shall implore the fates
soon to find myself close to you,
from your eyelids
the rain to drain
and your body
with perfumes to drape.
Thus , the rough rugged road
in the twilight of my forgotten memories
where unwelcome shadows dwell
shall I dissolve.

Sheltering sky

In this world of gridlocked dreams
insecurity runs wild
loneliness wears its Sunday best
and the soul, like a threadbare rag,
drifts from place to place
searching for something to hold on to...
But it's bitter cold!
Still I...I have you my sheltering sky!
To lightly lean on
to carry me along in your caress of a breeze
to tirelessly steer me to the world
I dream of...
the world of benevolence and light!

www.ingramcontent.com/pod-product-compliance
Lightning Source LLC
Chambersburg PA
CBHW031943070426
42450CB00006BA/872